Quran Story

The Story of the Prophet Musa عليه السلام

By
Saniyasnain Khan

Illustrated by Gurmeet

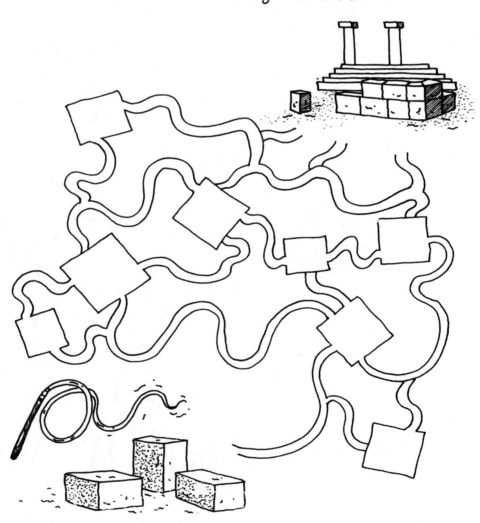

Goodwordkidz

First published 2003   Reprinted 2018 © Goodword Books 2018
Goodword Books
A-21, Sector 4, Noida-201301, India
Tel. +9111-46010170, +9111-49534795, Mob. +91-8588822672
email: info@goodwordbooks.com, www.goodwordbooks.com, Printed in India

This story starts long long ago—in fact, about 3000 years ago in Egypt.

Do you know where Egypt is? Find it on this ancient map. Also try to find out if you can visit Egypt and other places on the map by following the maze.

2

The kings of Egypt were powerful rulers called Pharaoh or Firawns. They built huge monuments called pyramids.

Find out if any of these paths lead to the pyramids.

Start

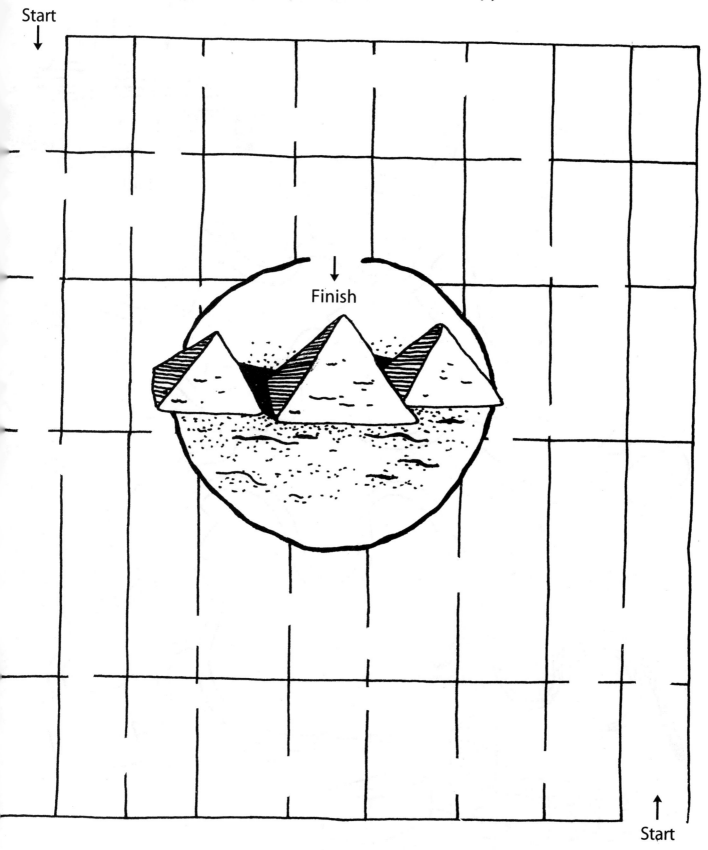

Finish

Start

3

The king or Firawn, at that time was a very cruel man. He had enslaved the people of the tribe of the children of Israel. They were forced to build palaces and other buildings.

Help them take these stones to where a palace is being built.

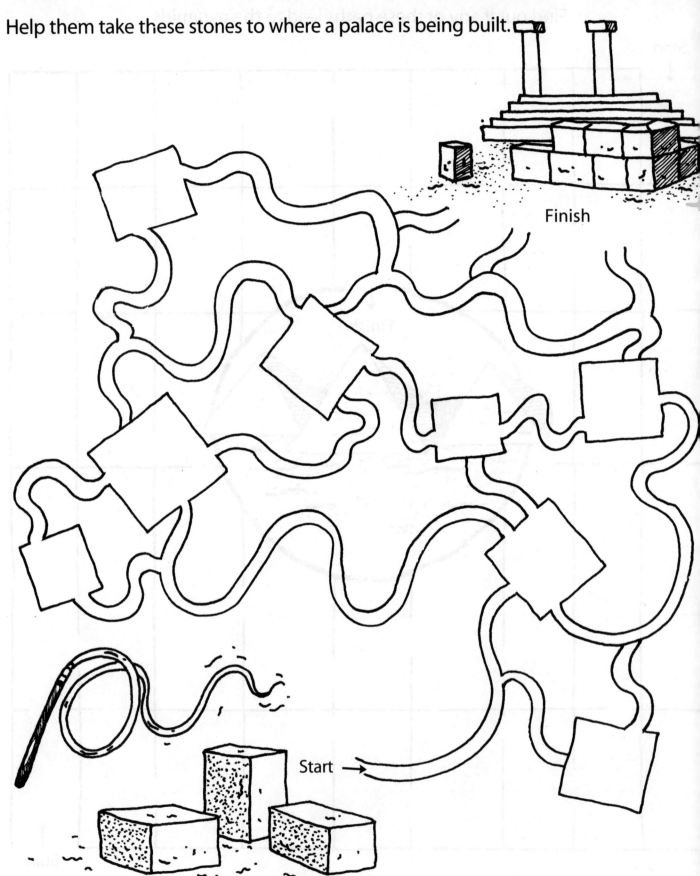

Finish

Start →

One day, a court soothsayer told Firawn something that enraged him.

Trace the maze and write down the words to find out what he said.

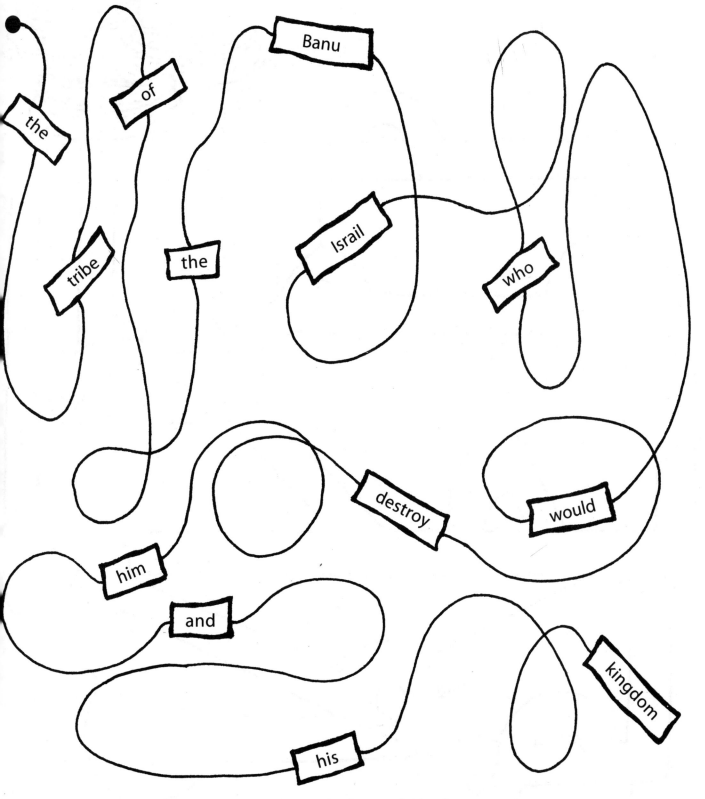

The soothsayer told him that that year a boy would be born among ____ ____ ____

____ ____ ____ ____ ____ ____ ____ ____ ____ ____ .

The cruel Firawn ordered all the newborn boys of the tribe to be killed.

Can you trace your way to these newborns?

Finish

Start

During these terrible times a pious woman called Yukabid of children of Israel gave birth to a beautiful boy who was named the Prophet Musa (or Moses) علیه السلام. She was told by Allah that this was a very special child, who would one day become a great prophet.

Find your way to the baby's cot.

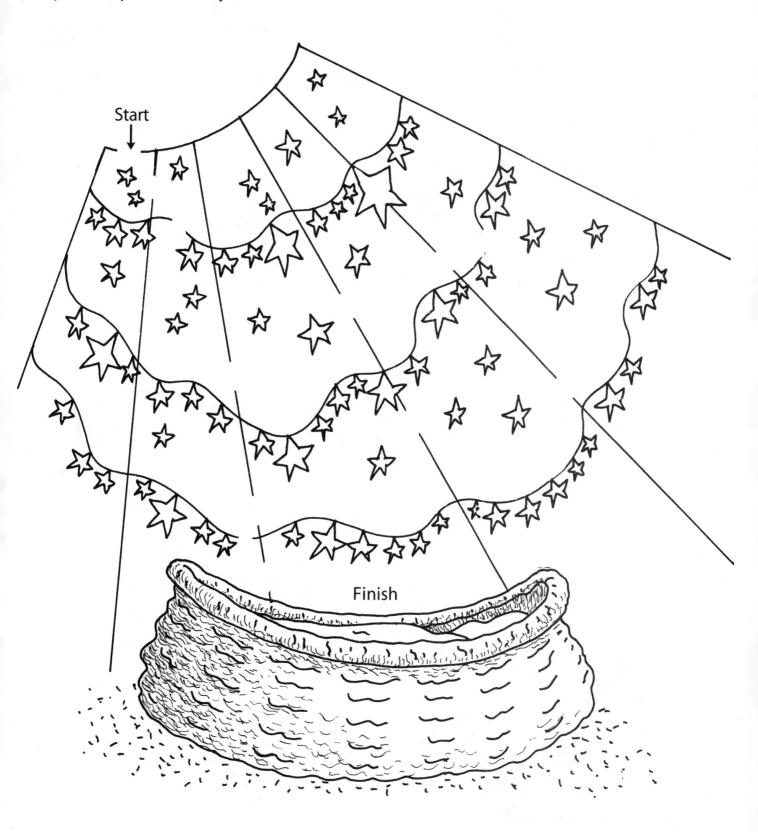

Start

Finish

7

Through Egypt flows a great river called the Nile.

Cross the Nile in this maze as you go from start to finish.

Start

Finish

8

Allah inspired Yukabid to put the baby in a box and cast the box into the river Nile with the promise that her baby would be safe.

Can you find your way through the waves to the shore?

Finish

Start

Carried by the waves the box stopped at a bank near the royal palace. There it was picked up and brought to the queen who was a kind-hearted woman.

Trace the way from the box to the bank.

Finish

Start

10

Quran Story Mazes: The Prophet Musa

The Prophet Musa ﷺ was brought up in the King's palace under the kind eye of the queen. He grew up to be a strong and handsome youth.

Try this palace maze.

Finish

Start

One day the Prophet Musa ﷺ accidently killed one of the king's followers. He had not meant to do so, but Firawn decided to slay him. So, the Prophet Musa ﷺ left the city. He travelled many days to reach Madyan.

Follow the trail of stars to get to Madyan.

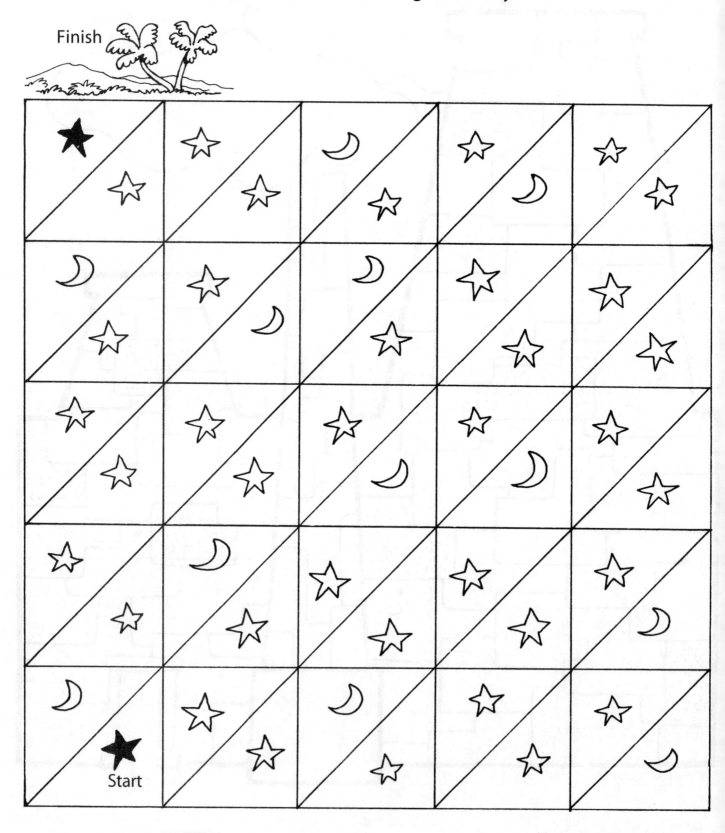

There the Prophet Musa ﷺ met the Prophet Shuyab ﷺ and married one of his daughters.

Do not tread on any flower as you solve this maze.

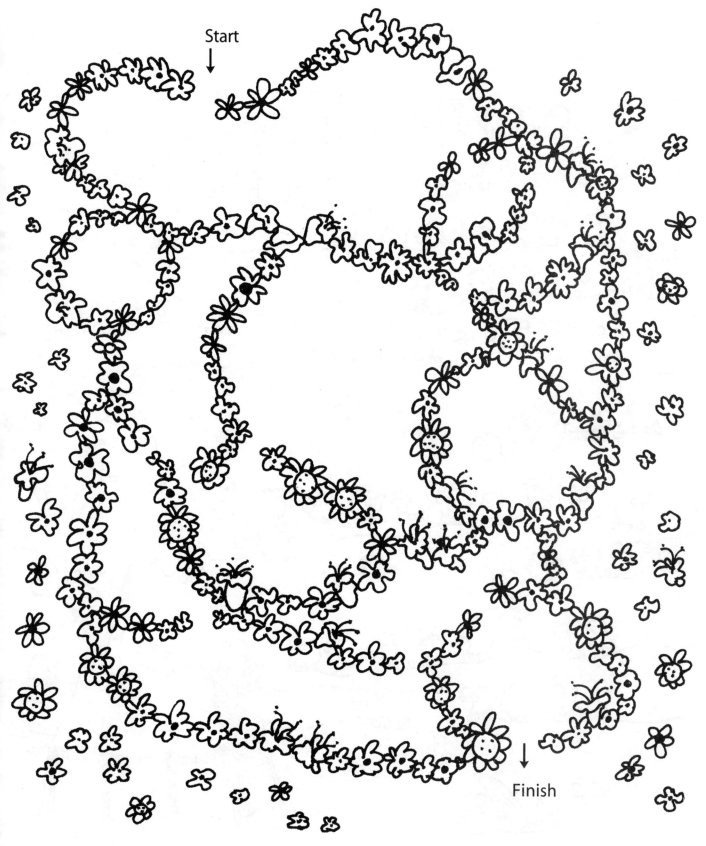

Start

Finish

The Prophet Musa ﷺ spent about eight years in the beautiful and peaceful valley of Madyan.

You will pass through a flock of sheep as you follow this maze.

Finish

Start

14

The Prophet Musa ﷺ decided to return to Egypt with his family. They slowly travelled towards Mount Sinai.

Can you find your way to Mount Sinai?

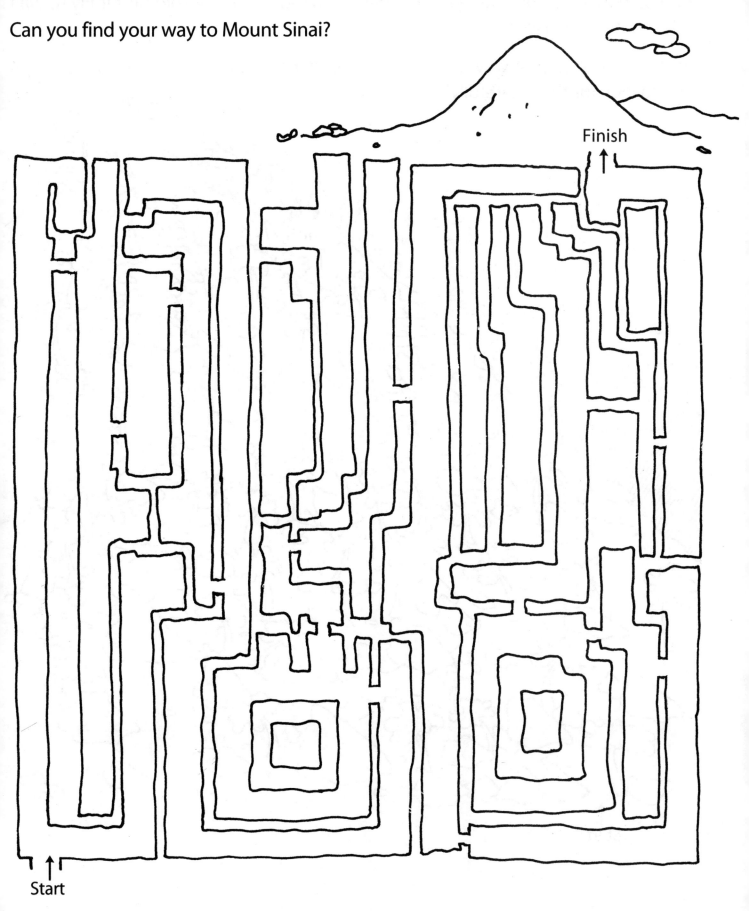

Finish

Start

It was a cold winter evening and they seemed to have lost their way. Then the Prophet Musa ﷺ noticed a fire far away on the side of a mountain. He told his family to wait and went to have a look.

See if you can find your way to the fire. Remember, the gaps are narrow so you might have to look for them carefully!

Finish

Start

As the Prophet Musa ﷺ reached the source of the light, he heard a voice calling out from above a tree.

Follow the maze and write down the words to find out.

Start

Musa

I

am

mighty

the

Allah

the

wise

one

Finish

The voice said, "_____, _____ _____ _____, _____ _____, _____ _____ _____."

Allah gave the Prophet Musa ﷺ wisdom and the gift of performing miracles. Allah told him that He had chosen him as his messenger and commanded him to go with His signs and give His message to Firawn, who had made himself a tyrant in the land.

Make your way to Firawn's palace.

Finish

Start

Inspired by Allah, the Prophet Musa ﷺ with his brother Harun reached Firawn's court but Firawn rejected him outright. To convince him, the Prophet Musa ﷺ threw down his staff and it turned into a huge snake. Then he drew out his hand from his armpit and it was shining brightly.

Try going from head to tail of this big snake.

Start

Finish

Firawn called his best magicians to outdo the Prophet Musa ﷺ. They threw down their magic ropes and sticks. These now looked like live snakes.

Try not to get bitten by a snake as you solve this maze.

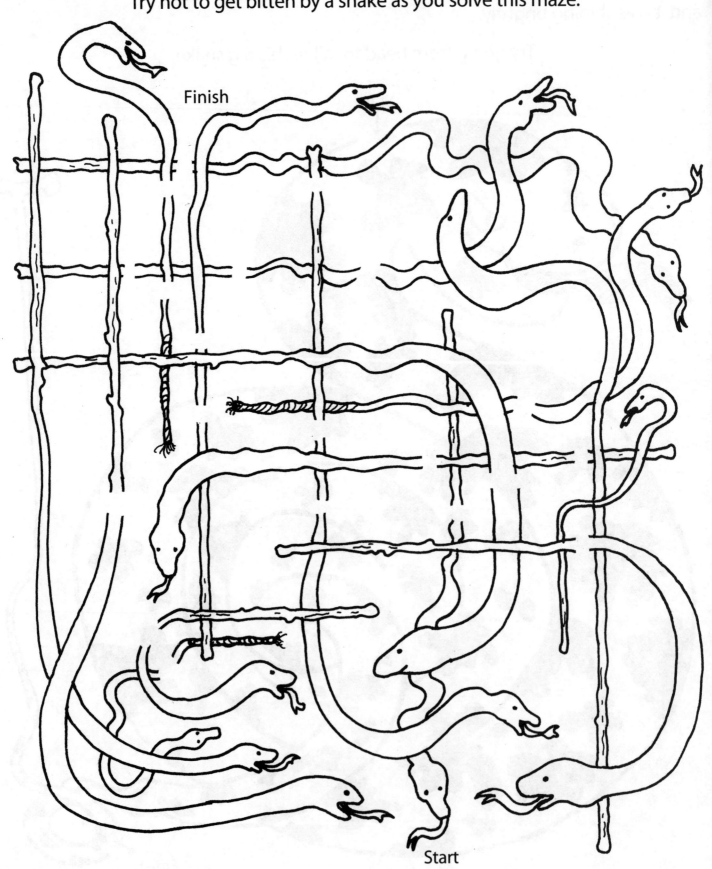

Finish

Start

The Prophet Musa عليه السلام threw down his staff and it became a giant snake which ate up all the other snakes. The magicians fell down on the ground in skew awe of the Prophet Musa عليه السلام.

Go from head to tail of the huge snake to find out what they exclaimed.

We

believe

in

the

lord

of

Musa

and

Harun

The magicians exclaimed,

"_____ _____ ____ _____ _____

_____ ____ ____ ____ _____."

The evil Firawn grew even more angry and redoubled his cruelties on the people of the children of Israel. The Prophet Musa ﷺ was finally commanded by Allah to leave Egypt along with all his people. So one night, the people of the children of Israel set out secretly in a caravan with their flocks and all their belongings. In this maze one of the path leads to safety. On the other you will get lost.

Find out which is the right path.

When Firawn learnt of their escape, he set out with his huge army with its many chariots, horsemen and soldiers to punish the children of Israel.

Can you tell which one of these paths would take Firawn's army to the fleeing people?

Firawn's huge army created a great cloud of dust. As the soldiers came nearer, the sight of the giant cloud terrified the children of Israel.

Can you find your way in all this dust?

Start

Finish

The children of Israel were trapped between Firawn's army and the sea with nowhere to go.

Which of these paths will take Firawn to the terrified people?

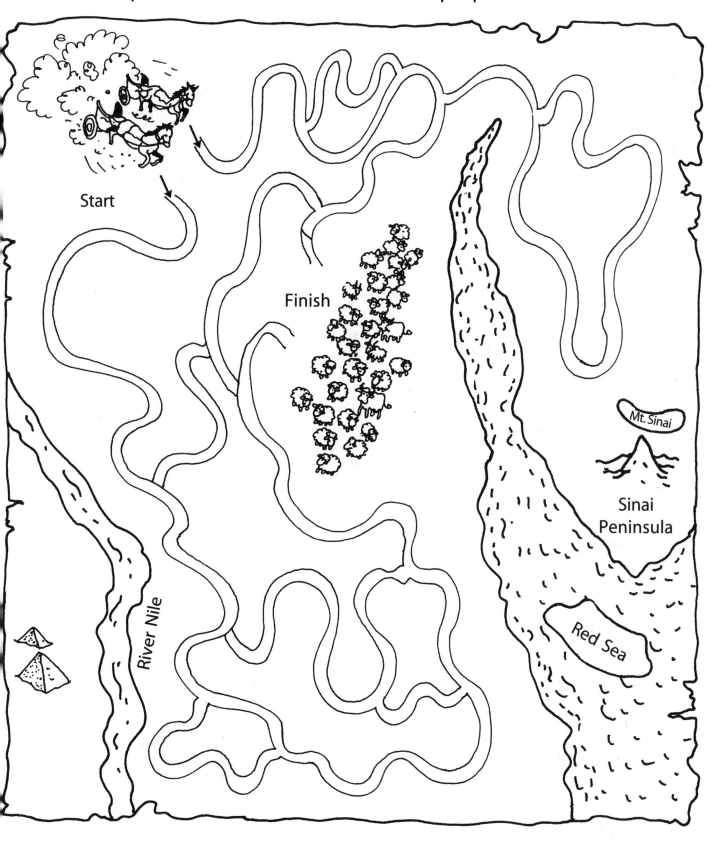

As the troops of Firawn approached and the people had nowhere to go, Allah spoke to the Prophet Musa ﷺ .

What did He tell the Prophet Musa ﷺ? Follow the maze and write down the words to find out.

Sea

the

strike

to

his

with

staff

Allah told him ____ ___ ___ ___ ___ ___ ___ .

As the Prophet Musa ﷺ struck the sea with his staff, a great miracle took place. The waves of the sea began to split into two halves. What an amazing scene!

Can you swim through these waves?

Start

Finish

A path across the sea opened up and the Prophet Musa ﷺ and his people thanked Allah as they safely crossed over.

Can you make your way through this caravan?

Firawn decided to follow the Prophet Musa ﷺ and his people. But when Firawn and his army were half way across the sea, the waves, standing like two walls, now turned back into water and fell on them. Firawn and all of his soldiers were drowned.

See if you find your way to safety.

Start

Finish

The children of Israel safely reached the Sinai Peninsula and settled there.

Here is a happy Sinai landscape. Help a bee find its partner.

Start

Finish

30

You now know about the Prophet Musa ﷺ. The Quran tells us about many other prophets. You might know about some of them. Follow the maze and write down the small letters to find out the names of some of the prophets whose stories are found in the Quran.

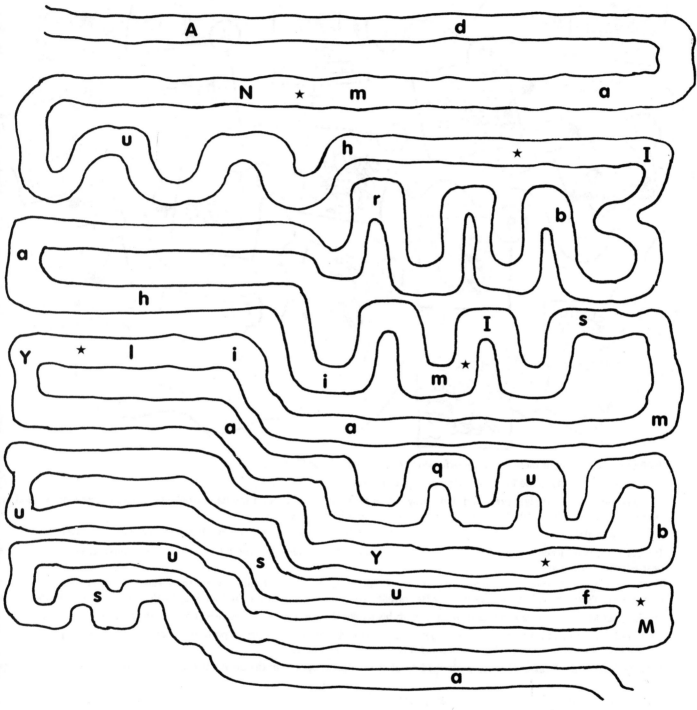

1. The Prophet **A** _ _ _ ﷺ.

2. The Prophet **N** _ _ _ _ _ _ ﷺ.

3. The Prophet **I** _ _ _ _ _ ﷺ.

4. The Prophet **I** _ _ _ _ _ ﷺ.

5. The Prophet **Y** _ _ _ _ _ ﷺ.

6. The Prophet **Y** _ _ _ _ _ ﷺ.

7. The Prophet **M** _ _ _ ﷺ.

Trace the maze and number the pictures. Can you narrate this story using these pictures? You may take the help of the text below.

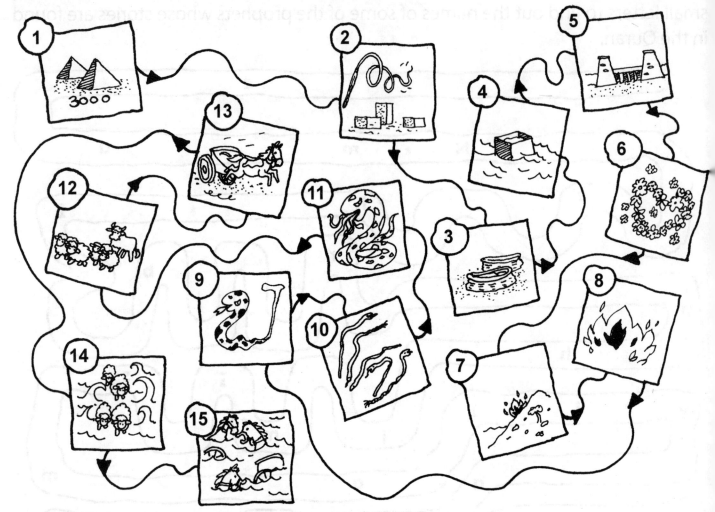

1. 3000 years ago in Egypt there ruled powerful kings called Pharaohs or Firawns.

2. The Firawn had enslaved the Banu Israil (the people of Israel).

3. One day the court soothsayer predicted that a boy would be born in the tribe of the Banu Israil who would destroy Firawn and his kingdom. The evil ruler ordered that all newborn boys of the tribe be killed.

4. Allah inspired Yukabid, the mother of a newborn boy named Musa ﷺ, to put her baby in a box and cast it into the river Nile.

5. The baby boy was picked up near the royal palace and brought to the queen. She brought up the Prophet Musa ﷺ and gave him the best education and care.

6. The Prophet Musa ﷺ grew up to be a strong and handsome man. One day, without meaning to he killed one of Firawn's follower. To escape Firawn's wrath, he had to leave the city. He travelled to Madyan and met the Prophet Shuyab. He married one of his daughters.

7. The Prophet Musa ﷺ decided to return to Egypt with his family. On the way, at Mount Sinai, he was attracted by a fire.

8. Allah spoke to him and made him his messenger. He gave him wisdom and miracles to perform. He commanded the Prophet Musa ﷺ to take His message to Firawn, who had become a tyrant in his own land.

9. In Firawn's court the Prophet Musa ﷺ performed miracles to impress upon him the power of Allah. He made his staff turn into a huge snake.

10. To counter the Prophet Musa ﷺ, the court magicians turned their ropes and sticks into serpents.

11. The Prophet Musa ﷺ threw his staff down and it became a giant snake, which ate up all the other snakes. The magicians were wonder struck and exclaimed that they believed in the Lord of the Prophet Musa ﷺ.

12. The enraged Firawn redoubled his cruelties to the Banu Israil. Therefore, one night, they secretly left in a caravan.

13. The angry Firawn, on learning of their escape, came after them with his huge army.

14. Allah told the Prophet Musa ﷺ to strike the sea with his staff. Amazingly, the sea parted and the people were able to cross it safely into the Sinai peninsula.

15. Firawn tried to follow them but the waves turned back into water and he and his huge and the powerful army were all drowned.